FOREWORD

Historical figures create a mystical imagination in the mind of the reader. The absence of the past fascinates the thinker on how things were done back then.

This book takes an in-depth look into the life of Rutherford B. Hayes, the nineteenth president of The United States of America.

The content in this book have been compiled by the author from the public domain and do not in any way represent his opinion.

- SARFARAZ KARMALI

THE LIFE OF A PRESIDENT

19. Rutherford B. Hayes

Sarfaraz Karmali

1822 - 1893

RUTHERFORD B. HAYES

It is the desire of the good people of the whole country that sectionalism as a factor in our politics should disappear. They prefer that no section of the country should be united in solid opposition to any other section.

Fourth Annual Message

FAST FACTS

FULL NAME
Rutherford Birchard Hayes

BIRTH DATE
October 4, 1822

DEATH DATE
January 17, 1893

BIRTH PLACE
Delaware, Ohio

EDUCATION
Kenyon College (graduated 1842), Harvard Law School (graduated 1845)

RELIGION
Methodist

CAREER
Lawyer

POLITICAL PARTY
Republican

NICKNAME
"Dark-Horse President," "Rud"

MARRIAGE
December 30, 1852, to Lucy Ware Webb (1831–1889)

CHILDREN
Birchard Austin (1853–1926), James Webb Cook (1856–1934), Rutherford Platt (1858–1927), Joseph Thompson (1861–1863), George Crook (1864–1866), Fanny (1867–1950), Scott Russell (1871–1923), Manning Force (1873–1874)

INAUGURATION DATE
March 5, 1877

DATE ENDED
March 4, 1881

PRESIDENT NUMBER
19

BURIAL PLACE
Spiegel Grove State Park, Fremont, Ohio

OVERVIEW

The policies of Rutherford B. Hayes, America's nineteenth President, began to heal the nation after the ravages of the Civil War. He was well suited to the task, having earned a steadfast reputation for integrity throughout his career as a soldier and a statesman. Upstanding, moral, and honest, Hayes was elected after the most lengthy, bitterly disputed, and corrupt presidential election in history.

LIFE IN BRIEF

The policies of Rutherford B. Hayes, America's nineteenth President, began to heal the nation after the ravages of the Civil War. He was well suited to the task, having earned a steadfast reputation for integrity throughout his career as a soldier and a statesman. Upstanding, moral, and honest, Hayes was elected after the most lengthy, bitterly disputed, and corrupt presidential election in history.

Hayes's father ran a successful farm and whiskey distillery in Ohio but died ten weeks before Rutherford was born. Raised by his single mother, Rud developed a very close relationship with his brilliant sister, Fanny Hayes, who encouraged him to achieve the prominent career denied to her because she was a woman. With the help of his wealthy uncle, Sardis Birchard, Hayes went to Harvard Law School and then made a name for himself as a successful criminal defense lawyer in Cincinnati. There he married Lucy Ware Webb. Lucy advocated temperance and abolition, and was a strong Methodist who placed more emphasis on good works than on being "born again." Without nagging, she influenced her husband. After marriage he became a stronger antislavery advocate and a teetotaler following his move to the White House, and he regularly attended religious services with Lucy, though he never joined a church.

Patriot of the Union

When the Civil War broke out, Hayes was already nearly forty-years old and the father of three with a fourth on the way. Nevertheless, he was one of the first three-year volunteers, stating that he would rather die in the conflict than live having done nothing for the Union. Using his political connections, Hayes was appointed a major in the 23rd Ohio Volunteers. An officer with no military experience, he learned quickly, worked hard, and with his "intense and ferocious" demeanor on the battlefield gained the respect of the enlisted men and his superiors. At the Battle of Opequon Creek, for example, Hayes led the charge through a morass that turned the tide of battle. Wounded five times in the war, Hayes kept leading his men into battle, and by the end of the conflict he was a brigadier general, and later breveted major general for "gallant and distinguished services." While campaigning in the Shenandoah Valley in 1864 he was nominated in Cincinnati for the U.S. House of Representatives. Hayes refused to return to take to the stump, stating that "an officer fit for duty who at this crisis would abandon his post to electioneer for a seat in Congress ought to be scalped." That statement was worth all the speeches he could have made. Hayes was elected and the war was over before the first session of his Congress met on in December 1865.

Road to the White House

After the Civil War, Hayes served as member of the U.S. House of Representatives (1865-1867) and then as governor of Ohio (1868-1872, 1876-1877). By 1876, Republicans recognized that the scrupulous Hayes—a war hero from a populous swing state and a candidate acceptable to the major factions in the Republican Party - was presidential material. "Availability" secured Hayes the nomination, but he faced a tough campaign. The nation was in the midst of an economic depression, the Grant administration was tarnished by scandals, and Democratic opponent Samuel J. Tilden of New York was a superb political organizer with a reform reputation. On Election Day, Tilden rolled up a plurality of 250,000 votes, but the vote in three southern states was close enough for both Republicans and Democrats to claim them and with those states the presidency. To decide who carried those states, Congress set up a special commission which awarded the disputed Electoral College votes to Hayes, making him the winner. Outraged and frustrated, Democrats dubbed Hayes "Rutherfraud" and "His Fraudulency."

The Hayes Presidency

Hayes's inaugural address was conciliatory in tone and addressed specific problems. To alleviate hard times, he backed existing legislation that called for the nation's return to the gold standard in 1879. To eliminate political corruption, he advocated a nonpartisan reformed civil service, observing that "he serves his party best who serves his country best." To conciliate the South, Hayes said it should have local self-government, but that those governments must obey the entire Constitution, including the Reconstruction amendments. Perhaps because Hayes, along with his comrade in arms William McKinley, had more combat experience than other Presidents, he wished to arbitrate disputes with other nations. He also congratulated the American people for the peaceful resolution of the recent disputed election.

As President, Hayes sought to implement his inaugural address. He had supported radical Reconstruction legislation which aimed to secure the rights of black citizens, but by 1877, Hayes believed that military occupation had bred hatred among southerners and had prevented the nation from healing itself in the aftermath of war. Actually, Reconstruction was virtually over when Hayes took office in March 1877, with federal troops protecting Republican governments only in New Orleans, Louisiana, and Columbia, South Carolina. It ended completely when, within two months of his inauguration, Hayes ordered those federal troops to their barracks, but only after Louisiana and South Carolina authorities pledged to respect the civil and voting rights of blacks. These promises were soon broken and the white supremacist Democratic Party asserted total dominance of the South. By the 1890s, the Democratic hold on the South resulted in a complete denial of voting rights for blacks until the 1960s.

Hayes was a patient and a gradual reformer. He feared that sweeping changes were often not lasting and was satisfied with smaller incremental gains. He had great faith in education as the keys to prosperity and harmonious relations among diverse racial and ethnic groups. He did not attempt to reform the entire civil service, but concentrated on one major office, demonstrating that open competitive examinations did, in fact, reap better workers. He did not attack all spoils-minded senators but only the imperious and obnoxious Roscoe Conkling of New York. The death of Abraham Lincoln, the impeachment of Andrew Johnson, and the failures of Ulysses S. Grant had left the presidency in a weakened state. Hayes helped to restore prestige to the office by defeating Conkling and the idea of "senatorial courtesy," which claimed for senators the right to appoint civil servants in their states. He also defeated an attempt by the Democratic-controlled Congress to force him to accept unwanted legislation by attaching amendments - riders—to necessary appropriations bills. By the time Hayes left office, senators could suggest but not dictate the appointment of officers, nor was the President's veto power destroyed. Hayes helped restore prestige to the presidency, heal the wounds left by the Civil War, and strengthen the Republican Party sufficiently to win the election of 1880.

In his very active retirement Hayes continued to struggle for equal educational opportunities for all children. He also was active in the prison reform movement.

LIFE BEFORE THE PRESIDENCY

Born on October 4, 1822 Rutherford Birchard Hayes, called "Rud" as a child, was named for his father and grandfather. His American roots traced back to 1680's New England. Five years before Rud's birth, his parents fled the poor economy there and resettled in Delaware, Ohio, just north of Columbus. They secured a farm, established a whiskey distillery, and built a house in town. But Rud's father died in July 1822, leaving Sophia Birchard Hayes—already mourning the recent loss of a daughter—with two children and a third on the way. The future President was born ten weeks after his father's death. He was often sick as an infant. When Rud was only two, just as his health improved somewhat, his nine-year-old brother drowned while ice-skating. Sophia was left with a daughter, Fanny, and a son Rud, who remained frail.

Although born in the shadow of tragedy, Rud enjoyed a comfortable, loving childhood. Sophia Hayes was religious, independent, and energetic; the widow faced her hardships with remarkable ability. Her younger brother, Sardis Birchard, after sewing wild oats, settled down as a merchant in Lower Sandusky, Ohio, where he prospered and, though absent, served as a surrogate father for Fanny and Rud. Sophia took in two lodgers and, with the farm leased for a share of the crops, managed to make ends meet. She was extremely protective of Rud, who was not allowed to play outside the family until he was seven or engage in rough sports until nine years of age. As a result Fanny and Rud were unusually close, playing together and nursing each other when ill. Sophia taught Rud to read and write, but through Fanny, who was exceptionally bright, he became acquainted with Shakespeare's plays and Sir Walter Scott's poetry. They also attended for a short time a newly opened publically supported district school. Rud later recalled: "The school was free to all and was crowded with scholars of all ages, from little folks of our own size up to young men grown. The school-master, Daniel Granger, was a little, thin, wiry, energetic Yankee, with black hair, sallow complexion, and piercing black eyes; and when excited appeared to us a demon of ferocity. He flogged great strapping fellows of twice his size, and talked savagely of . . . throwing them through the walls of the schoolhouse. He threw a large jack-knife, carefully aimed so as just to miss, at the head of a boy who was whispering near me." Despite the brief frightening experience with Granger, Rud regarded Joan Hills Murray, who ran a private grade school in Delaware, as his "first teacher." Both children studied hard and their uncle, Sardis Birchard, helped finance their later private schooling. Rud attended Norwalk Seminary in Ohio, then another private institution in Connecticut. He then enrolled in Kenyon College, at Gambier, Ohio, where he was named valedictorian of the class of 1842. In keeping with the ambitions and dreams of Fanny and Sardis for his future, Rud decided to pursue a legal career. He studied in a law office in Columbus for ten "vexatious and tedious" months before entering Harvard Law School, earning a bachelor of laws degree in 1845. He joined the Ohio bar that year and opened a practice in Uncle Sardis's town of Lower Sandusky (which within a few years was renamed Fremont).

Law Career and Marriage

Hayes's law practice got off to a sputtering start. Business was slow and the young lawyer was bored, restless, and—though he denied it—had symptoms of tuberculosis. After visits to New England and Texas, and seeking a fresh start, he moved to Cincinnati on Christmas Eve, 1849. In time, he made a name for himself in criminal law. Using his natural charm and his elite training, he defended society's outcasts, often managing to free them or save them from the gallows. He also had a full social life, calling on young women and joining clubs and societies. On Wednesday evenings, he was at the International Order of Odd Fellows; on Thursday, at the Sons of Temperance. Best of all were the Saturday night meetings of the Cincinnati Literary Club with its mix of intellectually stimulating discussions and oysters washed down with "liberal amounts of the local Catawba wine." More "exuberant members often adjourned to Gleissner's in the Over-the-Rhine area for some German lager." Hayes, a moderate reformer, was literally temperate in his use of alcohol and not a teetotaler.

While Hayes called upon and flirted with Cincinnati belles, he found himself more and more attracted to a girl from his home town of Delaware. In 1847, when he first saw Lucy Ware Webb at the Sulphur spring—a common meeting spot for young people — she was going on sixteen and, as he later remembered, "Not quite old enough to fall in love with." His mother had befriended Lucy's mother and wanted her daughter for her son. When Lucy was two, her father, a physician, died of cholera in Kentucky where he had gone to free slaves he had recently inherited. Widowed with three children, Lucy's mother when urged to sell those slaves to secure a decent income replied: "Before I will sell a slave I will take in washing to support my family." Like her parents, Lucy was strongly antislavery, supported temperance (unlike Hayes she was a teetotaler), and was a Methodist Christian who placed more emphasis on good works than on faith in doctrine. By the time Hayes set up shop in Cincinnati, Lucy Webb was nineteen and attending Cincinnati Wesleyan Female College, something novel for women in 1850. He looked her up, enjoyed her company, and, shortly after Lucy graduated from college that year, impulsively proposed to her in mid-1851. Lucy replied modestly, "I don't know but I am dreaming. I thought I was too light and trifling for you." He realized she was not light and trifling. The two, however, took their time setting a wedding date, doing so when Uncle

Sardis assured Hayes of his willingness to help them financially if necessary. Although Hayes had achieved some prominence as a court-appointed defender of notorious murderers, there were no lucrative fees involved and his income was hardly adequate to support a wife and family. The wedding took place in December 1852, and so began an equal partnership in a happy thirty-six year marriage. A degree of prosperity followed their wedding and ten months later they welcomed their first of eight children.

Taking up Antislavery Causes

Having regarded abolitionists as too radical, Hayes had been a moderately antislavery Whig in politics. But influenced by Lucy's antislavery convictions, Hayes in 1853 began to defend runaway slaves who had fled across the Ohio River from Kentucky. His defense in 1855 of Rosetta Armstead, a young girl, was most memorable. She was being escorted at the behest of her Kentucky owner through the free state of Ohio on the way to Virginia when she was detained by antislavery activists and freed on a writ of habeas corpus. Her former owner appeared and asked her before witnesses to choose between going with him or being free. She chose freedom, whereupon he had her arrested by a federal marshal as a runaway slave. Hayes, along with Sen. Salmon P. Chase and Judge Timothy Walker, defended Armstead. Not only was the slavery or freedom of a human being at stake but so were intriguing questions of law. Was Armstead a runaway since her owner brought her to Ohio? Did touching the free soil of Ohio automatically make one who was not a runaway free? Did her owner legally manumit her? Did her minor status affect her capacity to choose? Could a state court determine the legality of the imprisonment of anyone by a U.S. marshal? The Hamilton County Court of Common Pleas ruled that the right of transit of slave property through Ohio did not exist and that a state court on a writ of habeas corpus could, in fact, free a federal prisoner. The U.S. commissioner did not let the challenge to federal authority go unanswered. Armstead was rearrested and at the subsequent hearing, Hayes made the major argument for the defense; in Chase's words, Hayes "acquitted himself with great distinction." He castigated the owner for going back on his word and argued successfully that Armstead was not a runaway since her owner's agent brought her to Ohio. The commissioner agreed and Armstead was free.

After the Whig party broke up following passage of the Kansas-Nebraska Act of 1854 (which Hayes opposed), Hayes in 1855 helped mold the disparate opposition to the Democrats into the Ohio Republican party. Initially, however, he felt that the new party ignored the old Whig element, of which he was a part, and he became more involved with law and family than with politics. The Hayes' had a second son in March 1856, but in July that year, Hayes's beloved sister, Fanny, died from complications following childbirth. Hayes was deeply saddened by her death. She was the "dearest friend of childhood" and the "confidante of all my life." Fanny's death hit Hayes hard, but Lucy and their "fine little boys," as well as his profession and a newly kindled interest in politics, assuaged his grief. He supported the Republican candidate for President, John Charles Fremont—"For free states and against new slave states" —and was not discouraged by Fremont's defeat. He had faith that "right" would prevail. "However fares the cause," he declared, "I am enlisted for the war." In 1858, the Cincinnati City Council elected Hayes to complete the deceased city attorney's unfinished term. He then won election by the people to the post in 1859 and served until 1861.

Heroic Civil War Service

Hayes was willing to let the lower Southern states go when they seceded, following Abraham Lincoln's election in 1860, but he was outraged by South Carolina's April 12, 1861, attack on Fort Sumter. Aware that he had no military experience and was nearly forty-year old with three boys—and a fourth child on the way—Hayes drilled initially with a "volunteer home company" called the Burnet Rifles. He also thought the war would be short; by May

15, however, he realized the nation was facing a long, hard struggle and declared, "I would prefer to go into it if I knew I was to die ... than to live through and after it without taking any part in it." On June 7, the governor of Ohio made him a major in the 23rd Ohio Volunteers.

Hayes quickly earned the respect of the enlisted men and his superiors. He proved his mettle in battle and assured Lucy, "You need have no fear of my behavior in fight. I know somewhat of my capacity. It is all right." William McKinley, who enlisted in the 23rd Ohio (making it the only military regiment of more than one future President in American history), marveled that, "His whole nature seemed to change in battle. From the sunny, agreeable, the kind, the generous, the gentle gentleman ... he was, once the battle was on ... intense and ferocious." At the 1862 Battle of South Mountain in the Antietam Campaign, Hayes was at the head of the 23rd, spearheading the attack on the Rebel position in Fox's Gap. Two charges pushed the Confederates back, but just as Hayes ordered a third charge a musket ball fractured his left arm above the elbow, leaving a gaping hole. Hayes survived, thanks to the skill of his brother-in-law, Dr. Joseph Webb, his regimental surgeon. Lucy subsequently nursed Hayes and other wounded soldiers where they convalesced at Middletown, Maryland.

Hayes was promoted to colonel and from 1863 to 1865, regularly commanded a brigade; at times, he headed-up a division. In 1863 and 1864, Hayes's brigade conducted a series of dangerous, effective raids on rail lines and supply depots in Virginia. Later in 1864, Hayes's brigade participated in several battles in the Shenandoah Valley as part of George Crook's Eighth Corps of Philip Sheridan's Army of the Shenandoah. Hayes especially distinguished himself in the retreat after the defeat at Second Kernstown (July 24, 1864), and by leading the decisive charge through the mud of Rosebud Run at the victory of Opequon Creek (September 19, 1864). At Cedar Creek (October 19, 1864), Hayes's division absorbed elements of the surprise Confederate attack and Hayes injured his ankle when his horse was shot out from under him.

He was then hit in the head by a spent ball that no doubt passed through someone else. His men assumed he had been killed and his death was reported in the press. For Lucy, these were agonizing times, writing at one point: "Could I only know that you will be returned to me!" Fortunately, she heard that Hayes had survived Cedar Creek before she read of his death. Cedar Creek was Hayes's last battle. He was later promoted to brigadier general, was mustered out of the Army on June 8, 1865, and was breveted major general for "gallant and distinguished services." Hayes was pleased to become a general but freely admitted he never fought a battle as one. As a citizen officer who helped make the Army of a free, democratic republic successful, he asserted with pride: "I was one of the good colonels in the great army."

Congressman and Governor Hayes

In July 1864, Republican friends in Cincinnati, Ohio, nominated Hayes for a seat in the U.S. House of Representatives and suggested he get a furlough to come home and campaign. Absorbed with the ferocious summer fighting, he refused, noting that "An officer fit for duty who at this crisis would abandon his post to electioneer for a seat in Congress ought to be scalped. You may feel perfectly sure I shall do no such thing." That statement was more effective politically than any stump speeches he could have made back home. He learned of his election to the Thirty-ninth Congress while campaigning with General Philip Sheridan in the Shenandoah Valley that October. His term began on March 4, 1865, but the first session of that Congress did not meet until December 4, 1865. In the meantime, Lee surrendered to Grant on April 9, 1865, and Lincoln was assassinated five days later. With the war over, Hayes resigned from the Army in June, four years and a day after he took up arms.

Although being a congressman had its rewards, Hayes missed his family, which during four years of war he had seen only intermittently. He attended Congress faithfully, spoke rarely and supported Radical Reconstruction measures. In keeping with his literary, historical and intellectual interests, he made a significant contribution as chair of the Joint Committee on the Library by securing a $100,000 appropriation for the books and papers of Peter Force, the Washington printer and journalist.

He was reelected to the House in 1866, but resigned in 1867 to run for governor of Ohio. Hayes took the unpopular stand of supporting an amendment to the Ohio constitution giving voting rights to African-Americans. While the Democrats appealed to racial prejudice, Hayes accused them of treason, eking out a victory by less than 3,000 votes. But the Democrats won control of the Ohio state legislature and the suffrage amendment was lost. Nonetheless, the governor enjoyed life in Columbus, was reelected to a second term, and served from 1868 to 1872. His most important accomplishment was the ratification of the Fifteenth Amendment, eliminating race as a qualification for voting. He was also largely responsible for the establishment of Ohio State University, for an Ohio Geological Survey, and for appointing nonpartisan boards to oversee state institutions. Hayes supported Ulysses S. Grant for a second term in 1872 and, to strengthen the Republican ticket, ran for Congress. While Grant triumphed, Hayes lost. Retiring from politics, Hayes then moved to Fremont to help his Uncle Sardis, who was failing, manage his investments. Sardis died in 1874 leaving Hayes the bulk of his estate.

CAMPAIGNS AND ELECTIONS

The Campaign and Election of 1876:

By 1875, the Republican Party was in trouble. A severe economic depression followed the Panic of 1873 and scandals in the Grant administration had tarnished the party's reputation; falling crop prices, rising unemployment, and corruption in high places boded ill for the Republicans. Ohio Republicans turned to Hayes, their best vote-getter, to run against the incumbent Democratic governor. Once again, Hayes won a close race, with 5,544 votes out of almost 600,000 cast, and was immediately spoken of as a contender for the 1876 Republican presidential nomination.

As the favorite son of Ohio, Rutherford B. Hayes had much in his favor. Both regular and reform Republicans liked him. He was a war hero, had supported Radical Reconstruction legislation and championed Negro suffrage, and came from a large swing state. His reputation for integrity was excellent and his support of bipartisan boards of state institutions endeared him to reformers. Hayes realized that "availability" was his greatest strength. Distasteful to no one, he was the second choice among the supporters of the other leading candidates. Nevertheless, Hayes insisted on a united Ohio delegation and did nothing to lessen his availability. Moreover, the 1876 Republican convention was in Cincinnati, which teemed with Hayes supporters. "Availability" did work for Hayes. James G. Blaine, the frontrunner and the favorite of partisan Republicans, was tarnished by allegations of corruption; Oliver P. Morton, the favorite of Radicals, was in ill health; Benjamin H. Bristow, the favorite of reformers was anathema to Grant, Roscoe Conkling, the quintessential spoils politician, was unacceptable to reformers and to Blaine, and none of these candidates could muster the votes of the majority of the convention. By the fifth ballot, Hayes had picked up votes; by the seventh, he had clinched the nomination.

The Republicans faced a very difficult campaign. The Democratic candidate, Samuel Jones Tilden, governor of New York, had strong reform credentials. He had helped bust the infamous Tweed Ring, a corrupt group of Democrats that had been running New York City for years, and then smashed the state's corrupt canal ring. In addition Tilden was a superb political organizer and the Democrats in the South were certain to use violence to keep black and white Republicans from voting. Finally, the Republicans had been in power for a long time, were hurt by scandals, and hard times gripped the economy. There was strong sentiment to throw the ruling party out.

In that era, overt campaigning by the presidential candidate himself was largely frowned upon. Beyond publishing an acceptance letter, candidates were not supposed to demean themselves by campaigning—the office should seek the man. Not only were candidates mute, national committees were virtually powerless. Presidential campaigns were conducted by state and local party organizations headed usually by senators and congressmen. In his acceptance letter, Hayes called for a reform of the civil service and pledged to serve only one term, lest patronage be used to secure his reelection. He also backed the resumption of specie payments (return to the gold standard) as scheduled for 1879. Most importantly, he was a supporter of honest and capable local government in the South, as long as it respected the constitutional rights of all citizens.

The Disputed Election of 1876 to 1877

The election proved to be the longest, closest, most hostile, and most controversial - up to that time—in the history of the United States. Hayes knew it would be close and predicted that if he were defeated it would be "by crime—by bribery, & repeating" in the North and by "violence and intimidation" in the South. Early returns on the telegraph from both Ohio and New York showed Tilden in the lead, and Hayes went to bed convinced he had lost.

The next day, however, Hayes learned that he had carried the Pacific Slope and that both parties claimed to have carried Florida, Louisiana, and South Carolina. Tilden had a plurality of 250,000 in the popular vote and was one electoral vote shy of the majority needed to win the presidency. But if Hayes carried Florida, Louisiana, and South Carolina, whose official votes would be determined by Republican controlled returning or canvassing boards, he would win the presidency by one electoral vote. In those states, as well as in the rest of the South, intimidation kept black voters from the polls. Republicans asserted that had their votes been counted, Hayes would have carried the three disputed states as well as other southern states. Citing intimidation, the returning election boards in the disputed states invalidated enough Democratic votes for Hayes and the Republican Party to emerge victorious. A further complication arose in Oregon: Hayes carried the state, but one of his electors was a federal office holder and could not be an elector. He resigned his job after the election, but the Democratic governor of that state certified a Democratic elector in his place.

When electors met in state capitals to vote for president on December 6, 1876, both Republican and Democratic electors met in Florida, Louisiana, South Carolina, and Oregon, and cast conflicting votes. These were forwarded to Washington to be counted by the presiding officer of the Senate, Thomas W. Ferry, in the presence of both houses of Congress. Ardent Republicans claimed that Ferry had the right to decide which votes to count, but Democrats insisted that the joint session with its Democratic majority must decide. Congress resolved this impasse in the compromise (incidentally, the only important compromise in the disputed election) Electoral Commission Act passed in January 1877. It established a commission of five senators (three Republicans, two Democrats), five representatives (three Democrats, two Republicans), and five Supreme Court justices (two Republicans, two Democrats, and one political independent, Justice David Davis) which would decide what votes to count and thus resolve the election. Initially, Hayes did not like the Electoral Commission bill since it meant giving up on electoral "certainty." But when it passed, he realized it would enhance the legitimacy of the ultimate victor. Davis, however, disqualified himself after a monumental miscalculation by Tilden's corrupt nephew, Colonel William T. Pelton, who assumed that electing Davis as senator from Illinois with Democratic votes would purchase his support for Tilden on the Electoral Commission. Davis was replaced by a Republican, Joseph P. Bradley, giving Hayes's party an 8:7 edge. Bradley did have an independent streak, but in strict party votes Hayes was awarded the disputed states.

After the Electoral Commission awarded Louisiana to Hayes (which Tilden unofficially carried by 6,300 votes and where the Republican returning board threw out 15,000 votes of which 13,000 were Democratic), the Democrats knew that Hayes would win. Combining frustration and calculation, they then delayed the counting of electoral votes with frequent adjournments which threatened to plunge the nation into chaos by leaving it with no President on March 4. Those who calculated (as distinct from those who were irrationally angry) hoped to secure concessions from politicians close to Hayes. Among their objectives were the removal of the handful of troops that protected the remaining Republican state governments in New Orleans, Louisiana, and Columbia, South Carolina; a federal subsidy for the Texas & Pacific Railroad; and cabinet appointments for prewar Whigs accompanied with hints that if so rewarded, white southerners would be attracted to the Republican party. That southern

Democrats and Hayes's friends negotiated is a virtual certainty, but that they struck any "deal," "bargain," or compromise that offered anything beyond what Hayes promised to do in his letter of acceptance is very doubtful. Hayes and his representatives insisted that the troops would be withdrawn only when the civil and voting rights of black and white Republicans were respected. It is also clear that the southern negotiators had little or no control over the irrational filibusterers that prolonged the count. Samuel J. Randall, the Democratic Speaker of the House, realizing that creating chaos would backfire on the Democrats, ruled the filibusterers out of order and forced the completion of the count in the early hours of March 2, 1877. With 185 votes to Tilden's 184, Hayes was declared the winner two days before he became President.

It was, to say the least, a distasteful victory that left widespread hard feelings. Tilden had actually received a quarter million more popular votes than Hayes; this fact, coupled with the partisan work of the Commission, convinced Democrats that the recent political disgraces in Washington were far from over. The sneering Democratic press dubbed Hayes "Rutherfraud" and "His Fraudulency."

DOMESTIC AFFAIRS

Delivered on March 5—since March 4 was a Sunday—Rutherford B. Hayes's inaugural address tried to calm the nation and make clear his main policy concerns. According to the new President, "The fact that two great political parties have in this way settled a dispute in regard to which good men differ as to the facts and the law . . . is an occasion for general rejoicing."

Above all, Hayes wished to heal the wounds left by the Civil War: "Let me assure my countrymen of the Southern States that it is my earnest desire to regard and promote their truest interest, the interests of the white and of the colored people both and equally and to put forth my best efforts in behalf of a civil policy which will forever wipe out in our political affairs the color line and the distinction between North and South, to the end that we may have not merely a united North or a united South, but a united country."

Hayes wanted the South to have "wise, honest, and peaceful local self-government," but insisted that the interests of blacks and whites be guarded equally—that the Reconstruction amendments guaranteeing civil and voting rights must be obeyed. Hayes emphasized that the schoolhouse, not the railroad station, was the key to political stability and to economic prosperity in the South and elsewhere. He did not ask for railroad subsidies but called for federal aid for education, observing that "universal suffrage should rest upon universal education."

In addition to the disputed election and the South, Hayes addressed the problem of the depressed economy by returning to the gold standard, and the possibility of disputes with foreign powers, by embracing arbitration as Grant had with Great Britain in the 1871 Treaty of Washington. He also dealt with the problem of corruption by advocating a "thorough, radical, and complete" reform of the civil service. Although he realized he was elected by the "zealous labors of a political party," he reminded himself, in his most memorable words, "that he serves his party best who serves his country best."

Although Republican members of Congress universally supported Hayes while the election was in dispute, several party leaders, within hours of his inauguration, had become angered by his independence. In choosing his cabinet, Hayes ignored and offended leading Republican senators. He not only failed to appoint the political lieutenants of Blaine, Simon Cameron, and Roscoe Conkling, but also named William M. Evarts (who challenged Conkling's control of New York Republicans) as secretary of state, Carl Schurz (who bolted the Republican party to oppose Grant in 1872) as secretary of the interior, and David M. Key (who had been a Confederate and was a Democrat) as postmaster general. Hayes's appointment of Key was both a gesture of reconciliation and an attempt to attract white southern moderates to the Republican Party. Party leaders were enraged, but Hayes's demonstration that he was beholden to no one increased his credibility among reform-minded Republicans.

End of Reconstruction

The most difficult problem facing the nation, however, could not be postponed. While in Congress, Hayes had supported the radical reconstruction of the former Confederate states on the basis of universal male suffrage enforced by the military occupation of the South. As governor of Ohio, he had fought successfully for passage of the Fifteenth Amendment, eliminating race as a qualification for voting. Initially, the Republican Party, supported by blacks and a few whites, dominated southern state governments. Gradually, however, the Democratic party, by playing the race card and resorting to violence (the Ku Klux Klan is an example), gained control of state after state. By Election Day 1876, only Florida, Louisiana, and South Carolina had Republican governments. But on December 14, 1876, the Florida Supreme Court reversed the work of the state returning board and allowed the Democrats to take control of Florida on January 1, 1877. So by the time that Hayes took office, Reconstruction had already ended in the entire South except in Louisiana and South Carolina and in those states, extra-legal Democratic governments challenged the authority of the legitimate Republican governments. Their effective control was limited, however, to small areas surrounding state houses in the capitals of New Orleans and Columbia that were protected by small detachments of federal troops.

Reinforcing these Republican beachheads was not a viable option for Hayes even if he were so inclined. The 25,000 man U.S. Army was primarily deployed in the West and few troops were available. The Democratic House of Representatives had already refused to appropriate money to pay the Army as long as detachments protected Republican governments in the South. Hayes's mandate, to say the least, was shaky. All Democrats opposed military occupation and a large number of Republicans—including Hayes—had come to the conclusion that bayonet rule was counterproductive. Most northern whites were preoccupied with the economic problems of unemployment and falling farm prices, and were less concerned about violent acts of white southerners against blacks than they had been in the past. "Waving the bloody shirt" had lost some of its appeal twelve years after the war was over.

The question Hayes faced was not whether the troops should be removed but when they would be removed. Hayes, however, continued to be guided by what he said in his acceptance letter and reiterated in his inaugural address. He would be willing to remove the troops upholding Republican governments in Louisiana and South Carolina if leading Democrats in those states pledged to uphold the civil and voting rights of black and white

Republicans. The pledges were made, Hayes removed the troops, but the promises were soon broken. Over the next two decades, southern blacks were systematically disfranchised until virtually none could vote--a situation that persisted until well in the twentieth century. In addition, despite Key's appointment and his distribution of post office patronage, any hope of winning moderates to the Republican Party quickly evaporated. The color line prevailed and racism kept virtually all southern whites in the Democratic Party.

The depressed economy stagnated business, cut farm income, and had a devastating effect on labor. Less than three months after Hayes removed the troops in New Orleans, a general strike (the most widespread in American history) broke out in mid-July on trunk-line railroads between the northeastern seaboard and the Midwest. Wage cuts, on top of earlier reductions, led to the Great Strike of 1877, which began spontaneously on the Baltimore & Ohio (B&O) and quickly spread to other lines. Virtually none of the strikers were organized in any labor union and the strike grew without any leaders or organizations in control. Unemployed men and boys joined the strikers and rioting broke out at many points, especially in Baltimore and Pittsburgh. In Baltimore, men and boys stoned the Maryland militia, which opened fire, killing ten. An angry mob of 15,000 gathered outside the B&O depot where the militia, police, the mayor, the governor, and railroad officials were inside, and proceeded to burn passenger cars and part of the depot. In Pittsburgh, state officials called in the First Division of the Pennsylvania National Guard from Philadelphia to disperse the crowd blocking the departure of Pennsylvania Railroad freight trains. (The strikers allowed passenger trains with mail cars attached to depart on schedule.) The militia from Philadelphia dispersed the crowd temporarily by killing ten to twenty people and then retired to a nearby roundhouse for locomotives. An outraged crowd besieged the Philadelphia guardsmen and burned them out, killing five as they fled Pittsburgh. The mob then destroyed 104 locomotives, 2,152 railroad cars, and innumerable buildings.

Tom Scott, president of the Pennsylvania Railroad, urged Hayes to use federal troops to suppress the strike, but Hayes and his cabinet rejected Scott's plea to intervene on the side of railroad management. Hayes did not break the Great Strike of 1877. He used the Army not to operate trains but to keep the peace, and only when help was properly requested by state and local authorities who could no longer cope with riots. When railroad management claimed to be unable to transport the mail, Hayes refused to intervene to get it through. The huge disorganized strike was over by the end of the month, but the railroads had won a Pyrrhic victory. Workers gained more than they lost by fighting the wage cuts. The public tended to blame the railroads for the appalling conditions that caused the strike. The railroads attempted no further cuts, and by early 1880 had restored the cuts that precipitated the strike.

Money and the Economy

During the Civil War, the national debt had increased by a staggering 4,000 percent. Much of the conflict had been financed by long-term bonds that committed the government to repay investors the principal with substantial interest; when money could not be raised, the government paid for the war by printing "greenbacks," fiat paper money not directly backed by specie (gold or silver). Reflecting the perceived willingness or capacity of the federal government, at some future date, to redeem greenbacks in gold, their value dropped below par and fluctuated, bring gold out of circulation and the United States off the gold standard.

Advocates of inflation (usually Midwestern and southern farmers and businessmen who were in debt) wished to increase the number of greenbacks in circulation while creditors (often northeasterners whose banks provided them with an adequate money supply and who would profit from deflation) wished to return to the stability of the gold standard and redeem greenbacks at face value. The hard money (gold) people tended to see this conflict in moral rather than in economic terms, as a struggle between honest and dishonest money. Hayes, although a debtor himself (thanks to large investments in real estate) advocated hard money and believed the depression following the Panic of 1873 was aggravated by the threat of inflation that greenbacks represented. He wholeheartedly supported the 1875 Specie Resumption Act and, along with Secretary of the Treasury John Sherman, carefully built up the federal government's gold supply to redeem greenbacks by January 1, 1879. Because of Hayes's resolution and preparation greenbacks circulated at face value in gold by mid December 1878; by January 1879, more gold was exchanged for the convenient paper greenbacks than greenbacks were redeemed for heavy gold coins.

While Hayes and Sherman were preparing to return the United States to the gold standard, inflationists were shifting their support from the printing of greenbacks to the free (unlimited) coinage of silver at the ratio of 16 parts of silver to one part of gold. Since one part of gold was worth more than sixteen parts of silver, the silver coins would drive gold coins out of circulation and keep the United States off the gold standard. Under great pressure from inflationists and western silver miners, Congress, in 1878, passed the compromise Bland Allison Act over Hayes's veto. It required the secretary of the treasury to purchase at the market price $2 to $4 million of silver each month and mint that silver into dollars. Hayes saw to it that this Act did not have an inflationary effect. Sherman purchased the minimum $2 million of silver and redeemed silver dollars in gold coin upon request, and the United States went on the gold standard as scheduled. As Hayes predicted, prosperity returned with the return to the gold standard. Indeed, the last two years of Hayes's presidency were blessed by a stunning revival of business. No doubt, Hayes was lucky that the business cycle swung upward while he was President, but the stability and the predictability his policies provided enabled businessmen to calculate the costs of their future moves with a greater degree of accuracy, contributing to the economic recovery.

Fighting for Civil Service Reform

Hayes ruffled the feathers of Republican Party leaders by attempting to reform the nation's civil service. Government employees, especially those in the field service outside Washington, were appointed as much or more for their competence as political operatives than for their capacity as postmasters or revenue collectors. Civil servants were efficient political organizers but often neglected their official duties; at times, they were corrupt for the sake of party or personal financial gain. Assessments of civil servants were more important than corruption as a source of party revenues. Local, state, and federal politicians assessed from 2 to 7 percent of all civil servants' yearly salaries; those in lucrative positions (the legitimate fees collected by some officers exceeded Hayes's salary) paid more. Some recouped their assessment by accepting unlawful gratuities and bribes.

Moderate by nature, Hayes moved with caution and annoyed reformers who wanted sweeping changes, infuriating spoilsmen who wanted no reform. On June 22, 1877, Hayes issued an executive order prohibiting political assessments and forbade the management of political parties, conventions, and campaigns by civil servants. Hayes wanted to depoliticize the civil service but he did not want to destroy Republican Party organizations. Several Republican Party leaders in Congress, however, believed he was destroying their organizations and ignored his order.

The lieutenants of Senator Roscoe Conkling of New York were the most conspicuous in flouting Hayes's order. Chester A. Arthur, the collector of the Port of New York, ran the New York Customhouse, which collected 70 percent of the nation's revenue and was the largest federal office in the land. With Conkling's approval, Arthur (who was a reasonably efficient administrator and would later become the twenty-first President of the United

States) kept the customhouse in politics. Hayes wanted his order obeyed and decided to remove Arthur and his second in command. Hayes also wanted to reduce Conkling's political power; Conkling had been a rival for the nomination in 1876 and opposed Hayes's appointment of his political enemy, Evarts, to the cabinet. In addition, since the New York customhouse was so conspicuous, striking a blow there for reform would be an important symbolic act and, if reform had any merit, would have a practical effect on government service.

Hayes confronted Conkling in an era when the legislative branch wielded more power than the executive branch and routinely decided on civil service appointments in their home states and districts. He tried to replace Arthur with Theodore Roosevelt Sr., but Conkling rallied spoils-minded senators and blocked Roosevelt's confirmation by invoking "the courtesy of the Senate" (the notion that senators could dictate field appointments). Hayes bided his time and seven months later, on July 11, 1878, with Congress not in session, he suspended Arthur and replaced him with Edwin A. Merritt (Roosevelt had died) and named Silas W. Burt (an ardent reformer) as naval officer (the second in command at the customhouse). When the Senate reconvened in January 1879 Conkling again attempted to block Hayes's nominees. Hayes attacked, stating that the customhouse should be conducted on business principles and that Arthur and his men made it "a center of partisan political management." While most Republican Senators sided with Conkling, enough joined the Democrats (who were delighted by Republican divisiveness) to make Hayes victorious. Hayes insisted that the New York customhouse become a showplace for reform, giving Burt that responsibility. The customhouse was removed from politics and appointments were made based on merit, following open competitive examinations. The success of this initiative was a major factor in the passage of the Pendleton Civil Service Reform Act of 1883, two years following Hayes's departure from office.

Enhancing the Power of the President

In his struggle with Conkling and his cohorts in the Senate, Hayes regained the President's constitutional power over appointments. By the end of his administration, congressmen and senators could suggest whom they thought should be nominated for federal jobs at home, but they could not dictate appointments to Hayes. A more significant constitutional struggle occurred during the second half of Hayes's term in office. The Democrats won control of both houses of Congress in the 1878 elections. With the capacity to pass whatever appropriations bills they desired, the Democrats moved to force unwanted laws on Hayes by attaching legislation (called riders) to necessary money bills. This tactic was essentially a two-pronged assault on federal election enforcement laws. These laws were passed to protect the civil and voting rights of blacks in the South and to prevent fraud in northern cities. More fundamentally, the Democrats sought to use those riders to destroy the veto power of the President. They wanted to be able to intimidate black voters and to enable their city machines to cheat with no interference from the federal government in local, state, congressional, and presidential elections. They believed that repealing the election laws would bring them the presidency in 1880. In the ensuing "Battle of the Riders," Hayes relished the thought of being in combat once again and eagerly confronted the Democratic Congress.

Outraged by the rider tactic, Hayes called it "unconstitutional and revolutionary." Riders had been in the legislative bag of tricks since the days of Andrew Jackson, but they seldom affected major issues. For Hayes, the federal government had a duty to protect the rights of citizens at national elections; as President, he had a duty to prevent Congress from usurping his power to share in legislation. In April, May, and June, Congress passed appropriations bills with riders attached which Hayes promptly vetoed on two grounds: one, that every citizen has the right "to cast one unintimidated ballot and to have his ballot honestly counted," and two, that the riders were an unconstitutional attempt to force legislation on the President. The Democrats did not have the strength to muster a two-thirds majority to override the vetoes and Hayes's stirring veto messages (all of which he wrote himself) rallied public opinion and Republicans of all stripes to his side. The Democratic threat to shut down the government if they did not get their way failed miserably; they gave up and passed the necessary money bills. Rather than pave the way for Democrats to the White House they united Republicans who moved on to victory in 1880.

Treatment of Native Americans

Hayes's Indian policy was paternalistic, yet fundamentally decent. In the late nineteenth century, the federal government appropriated several million dollars annually for the support of Native Americans who had been forced off their lands and on to reservations which could not adequately sustain them. Hayes's secretary of the interior, Carl Schurz, reformed the Indian Bureau, the agency in his department that administered policies affecting Native Americans. Schurz cleaned out a ring within the bureau that had received gifts from Indian contractors and was defrauding both the Native Americans and the government.

Despite that excellent start, the removal of both the Nez Perce from their ancestral lands in eastern Oregon and of the Ponca from their reserve along the Missouri River in the Dakota Territory had tragic consequences. Both of these removals had been decided upon during the Grant administration and were carried out during the first three months of Hayes's term. The eviction of the Nez Perce from the Wallowa Valley led to a war that lasted from June to October 1877, during which time the Nez Perce out-maneuvered and out-fought the U.S. Army on a 1,700 mile retreat before they were forced to surrender in Montana just south of the Canadian border. The surviving Nez Perce were sent to the Indian Territory (present day Oklahoma). The Ponca, who did not resist, were also sent to the Indian Territory and would have been forgotten had not one of their chiefs, Standing Bear, tried to return to Dakota on foot in the winter with the corpse of his son, in hope of burying him with his forebears. He was arrested in Nebraska but his plight aroused enormous sympathy in the Northeast and sparked an Indian-rights movement that opposed removals of Native Americans. Responding to pressure but also recognizing the injustice and the high cost of the removal policy, the Hayes administration abandoned it. Hayes, Schurz, and the Indian Rights Association were humane in their paternalism but were not interested in preserving the culture of Native Americans. Indeed, Hayes believed acculturation was the best policy, that education coupled with learning to be a farmer, herder, teamster, etc. was in the Indian's best interest.

FOREIGN AFFAIRS

During the Hayes administration, the United States had few problems with foreign governments and little inclination to become an imperialist power. The problems involved Mexican bandits, who ignored the border between the United States and Mexico; Californians, who ignored the Burlingame Treaty and discriminated against Chinese residents of their state; and Ferdinand de Lesseps, who ignored Hayes and plunged ahead with his plans to build a Panama Canal.

Relations with Mexico and China

Three months after his inauguration, Hayes on June 1, 1877, ordered the Army to keep "lawless bands" from invading the United States, even if it had to cross into Mexico to punish these outlaws. Porfirio Diaz, who had assumed the Mexican presidency a month earlier (and would remain dictator until overthrown in 1911), protested and sent troops to the border to protect Mexico's sovereignty. Despite some bombastic talk, Diaz agreed to pursue bandits jointly with American troops; however, Mexico did not restore order on the border until three years later. With the incursions stopped, Hayes, on February 24, 1880, revoked his 1877 order permitting the army to follow outlaws into Mexico.

The 1868 Burlingame Treaty with China allowed unrestricted Chinese immigration to the United States. Chinese laborers, however, had been migrating to California since the 1849 gold rush and had drifted from the gold fields into railroad construction (the Central Pacific Railroad employed 10,000 from 1866-1869), agriculture, and urban jobs in factories, laundries, and homes. With the completion of the transcontinental railroad and the flood of cheaper manufactured goods from the East, California manufacturers cut costs by employing Chinese labor at low wages. The hostility of white laborers toward Chinese workers intensified during the depression that followed the Panic of 1873. The Great Strike of 1877 inspired anti-Chinese riots in San Francisco and a Workingmen's party wanting to "stop the leprous Chinamen from landing" expanded rapidly, becoming a major force in California politics by early 1878. At the 1878 California Constitutional Convention, it secured articles preventing the Chinese from voting and from working on local and state public works, or for any corporation operating under California law. These articles violated the federal Constitution and would be struck down by the federal courts, but they sent a message to Congress. The legislature responded with a bill that restricted incoming vessels to no more than fifteen Chinese passengers and violated the Burlingame Treaty, which allowed the immigration of Chinese and Americans to each other's country. Hayes vetoed the bill on March 1, 1878, and was bitterly denounced west of the Rocky Mountains.

Hayes, however, also responded to the pressure from the West Coast. He thought it best to discourage but not prohibit the influx of Chinese labor (which he noted was slowing down) and wanted negotiations with China to revise the Burlingame Treaty. Hayes appointed a commission to do so and by November 17, 1880, it had concluded immigration and commerce treaties with China. The immigration treaty enabled the United States to regulate, limit, and suspend, but not prohibit the coming of Chinese laborers. The commerce treaty prohibited the export of opium to either country. These treaties were ratified in 1881 after Hayes had left office. In 1882 Congress after attempting to suspend Chinese immigration for 20 years settled for ten years.

A Transoceanic Route

Schemes to connect the Atlantic and Pacific oceans through Mexico, Nicaragua, or Panama revived dramatically in 1879. In May of that year, the Congres International d'Etudes du Canal Interoceanique meeting in Paris was dominated by Ferdinand de Lesseps, the builder of the Suez Canal. With little thought and no research, he proposed that a sea-level Panama Canal be built by 1892 for $240 million. Aniceto Garcia Menocal, an American naval officer attending the congress, had surveyed the route, realized that a sea level canal was impossible, and advocated a Nicaraguan canal with locks. The gathering ignored the opinions of the expert engineers who were present, caught de Lesseps's vision, and endorsed his sea-level Panama proposal. De Lesseps immediately organized a private syndicate to build the canal, but throughout 1879 had little success in raising the necessary funds. Nevertheless, he remained optimistic, landed with an entourage at Colon, Panama (then part of Colombia), inspected the proposed route, and declared that the canal would be built. The plans and activities of de Lesseps concerned Hayes. The President would have been uneasy about any non-American inter-oceanic canal, but was doubly suspicious of a French project. Little more than a decade had elapsed since Napoleon III had tried to make Maximilian the emperor of Mexico. Hayes concluded that "The true policy of the United States as to a canal across any part of the Isthmus is either a canal under American control, or no canal." Following his inspection of Panama, de Lesseps toured the United States. He was feted in New York and received courteously by Hayes and the House Inter-oceanic Canal Committee. He addressed crowds on a whirlwind tour all the way to San Francisco and back, stressing that his was a private venture that in no way contradicted the Monroe Doctrine. Indeed, the French government assured the Hayes administration that it had nothing to do with the de Lesseps proposal. Hayes, however, was not reassured and in a special message to Congress on March 8, 1880, stated unequivocally that "The policy of this country is a canal under American control." A canal, Hayes proclaimed, "would be the great ocean thoroughfare between our Atlantic and our Pacific shores, and virtually a part of the coast line of the United States. Our merely commercial interest in it is greater than that of all other countries, while its relations to our power and prosperity as a nation, to our means of defense, our unity, peace, and safety, are matters of paramount concern to the people of the United States." In addition, Hayes anticipated the corollary to the Monroe Doctrine that Theodore Roosevelt would later proclaim, warning European investors not to look to their governments for protection. The United States would deem such intervention by European power as "wholly inadmissible. If the protection of the United States is relied upon, the United States must exercise such control as will enable this country to protect its national interests and maintain the rights of those whose private capital is embarked in the work." American capitalists were not attracted to de Lesseps venture. Hayes, no doubt, discouraged some; others were no doubt aware of the engineering absurdity of a sea-level Panama Canal. De Lesseps nonetheless forged ahead and claimed audaciously that Hayes's version of the Roosevelt Corollary guaranteed the political security of his proposed canal. De Lesseps returned to France in April 1880 and secured support from the French people. Despite Hayes's efforts, the project went forward but ultimately failed.

LIFE AFTER THE PRESIDENCY

The one-term pledge may not have been a wise political decision, but Hayes and Lucy had no regrets. Four years in the eye of the storm had been sufficient for them both. Alexander Stephens, once the vice president of the Confederacy, spoke for many when he said he had never seen a President leave power "so well spoken of." In contemplating retirement, Hayes determined that he would "promote the welfare and the happiness of his family, his town, his State, and his country." Hayes was an egalitarian and continued his support of social causes he had already embraced. His major emphasis was on universal tax-supported public education. He believed that the American government could be no better than its people and that its people could be improved morally and materially by education. He labored constantly to improve the educational opportunities for ordinary and gifted students from grade school to graduate school. He was the major dispenser of two educational funds to improve the education of southern blacks and whites, and fought for federal subsidies for children of all races in poor school districts. He believed that education would improve the economic status of the poor, would enlighten the intolerant, and provide the fair start in life envisioned by Lincoln—and the political equality declared by Jefferson—as part of everyone's birthright. Closely related to equality and education were Hayes's interests in prison reform and reducing crime. As governor and President, he was generous with pardons; in retirement, he opposed the death penalty. He had faith that criminals could be reformed through education, believing that crime was the product of poverty and desperation and could be reduced by a more equal distribution of wealth. Indeed, in the last decade of his life, he believed that the gap between rich industrial "kings" and laborers was the greatest problem facing the United States. He therefore favored the federal regulation of industry, industrial education—so that the rich would know what it meant to toil for a living—and confiscatory inheritance taxes to equalize wealth. He recognized social Darwinism for what it was. Unregulated competition, he believed, resulted not in the survival of the fittest but in the triumph of the most predatory corporations.

Hayes worked steadily for his causes but also enjoyed his beautiful Speigel Grove estate. Still, he felt "the soul" had left it when, in June 1889, Lucy died of a stroke. Hayes's only daughter, Fanny —named after his beloved sister—became the former President's companion, both at home and on his frequent travels. She remembered her father never traveling without several pictures of Lucy, which he would place about his hotel room or ship cabin. Hayes died of heart disease on January 17, 1893. A long funeral procession wound through the snowy Ohio countryside, led by President-elect Grover Cleveland and then Ohio governor William McKinley.

FAMILY LIFE

Reflecting Lucy's spirit, the Hayes White House was lively and informal. A superb contralto who accompanied herself on the guitar, Lucy filled the executive mansion with music. Vocalists and instrumentalists performed popular, folk, and classical music. On Sunday evenings, Lucy led a "sing" in the upstairs library. Carl Schurz often played the piano while friends from Ohio, members of the cabinet and Congress, and even Gen. William T. Sherman sang gospel songs. Among the steady stream of visitors was Thomas A. Edison, who demonstrated his latest invention, the phonograph, until 3:30 A.M. for the President, Lucy, and their guests. When the couple celebrated Christmas, they included everyone who worked in the White House. Fanny and Scott, their two youngest children, distributed presents to all the employees. The White House was often full of guests—indeed so full that one of their three older boys, upon returning home from college, had to sleep in a bathtub. The Hayeses most memorable social event occurred on December 30, 1877, when, surrounded by relatives, close friends, and the White House staff, they celebrated their twenty-fifth wedding anniversary and repeated their marriage vows.

There were, of course, formal entertainments which, despite the absence of wine and liquor, were lavish affairs. Lucy was not entirely comfortable at state dinners, which were too formal even with the Hayeses presiding. She did loosen up traditional New Year's receptions and formal levees (about once a month during the Winter social season) by inviting a bevy of young women from Ohio and elsewhere to put guests at ease. Among them was a future first lady, Helen Herron, who later married William Howard Taft. Lucy was accused of being a matchmaker and indeed two of her young friends did meet their husbands while visiting the White House.

The Hayes White House was western in its friendliness, good humor, openness, and unpretentiousness. Lucy inaugurated "informal" Saturday afternoon (3 to 5 P.M.) receptions in January 1878, with everyone "on an equal footing, the ladies generally appearing in street costume and always retaining their bonnets." During the winter, Lucy was always at home for her friends in Washington. William and Ida McKinley often dropped in and spent the evening in the Red Parlor with Lucy, surrounded by her young lady guests. With the house full of young people, "fun and frolic reigned all day and well into the night."

THE AMERICAN FRANCHISE

The Hayes presidency was an important chapter in African American history. Civil rights spokesman Frederick Douglass became the first black man to address a major party convention when he urged racial equality at the 1876 Republican convention which nominated Hayes. However, the backlash against newly freed blacks in the wake of Reconstruction's fall was tremendous in the South. The deal that gave Hayes the presidency secured the Democratic Party's near-total hegemony in the region—power that was largely maintained by denying African Americans of their civil and voting rights. This would culminate with the passage of Jim Crow laws in the 1880s and laws restricting the rights of blacks to vote in the 1890s. The result was a significant reduction in the size of the electorate.

Status of Native Americans

During his time in office, Hayes also voiced frequent support for Native American citizenship rights, also an unpopular cause at the time. Nevertheless, in the aftermath of Custer's 1876 defeat, the U.S. military continued its advances in Indian territory. In Montana, the Crow and Blackfoot were removed from their reservations. The Ute were moved off their lands in Colorado, and the Nez Perce were invaded after gold was discovered on the Salmon River in Idaho. Chief Joseph of the Nez Perce tribe fought valiant battles and eventually gave up, telling his people sadly in 1877:

"Hear me my chiefs. I am tired; my heart I am sick and sad. From where the sun now stands I will fight no more, forever."

Immigration from Asia

Asian immigrants began to find their way into America in the mid-nineteenth century, and by the time Hayes took office, resentment against them was strong as well. Competing for jobs with workers of German and Irish descent, Chinese immigrants were the subject of the first restrictive legislation on immigration, which Hayes vetoed in 1879 to broad public dissatisfaction. The President stuck to his guns, however, and pushed through his own plan that regulated Chinese immigration as opposed to banning it altogether. Two years after he left office, however, a ten-year ban on such immigration was enacted. This piece of legislation caused great resentment in China, which saw it as an example of racial discrimination, since immigrants from Europe were being welcomed by the millions.

IMPACT AND LEGACY

After finding "the country divided and distracted and every interest depressed," Hayes was proud that, upon leaving the White House, he "left it united, harmonious, and prosperous." He had found the Republican Party "discordant, disheartened, and weak," and left it "strong, confident, and victorious." He believed he had successfully confronted many issues: "The Southern question; the money question; the hard times and riots; the Indian question; the Chinese question; the reform of the civil service; the partisan bitterness growing out of a disputed election; a hostile Congress; and a party long in power on the verge of defeat." Apart from Lincoln's administration, Hayes boasted, "it would be difficult to find one which began with so rough a situation, and few which closed with so smooth a sea." Contemporaries were inclined to agree with Hayes. Henry Adams, a caustic critic of politicians who had dismissed Hayes in 1876 as "a third-rate nonentity" and voted for Tilden, acknowledged by 1880 that Hayes had conducted "a most successful administration." Mark Twain's prediction that the Hayes administration "would steadily rise into higher & higher prominence, as time & distance give it a right perspective," has not come to pass. Historians have blamed Hayes for the end of Reconstruction, for breaking the Great Strike of 1877, for championing the gold standard, for an Indian policy that aimed at acculturation, for negotiating a treaty that led to Chinese exclusion, and for being an inconsistent civil service reformer. It is unfair, however, to dismiss Hayes so summarily. Too often he has been measured against the ideals of a later era; his limited options have not been adequately understood and, at times, his actions have been misrepresented. He did not break the Great Strike, for example, and only sent troops to stop riots as any responsible President must when properly requested by state and local authorities. Additionally, Reconstruction was over, for all practical purposes, when Hayes took office. His only real choice was not whether but when troops had to cease protecting Republican governments in South Carolina and Louisiana. His opposition to inflation and support of the gold standard were accompanied by the return of prosperity. His Indian policy was indeed paternalistic and did aim at acculturation, but he stopped the removal of Native Americans to the Indian Territory and he embraced a policy of peace, which had its beginnings under Ulysses S. Grant, and not one of annihilation. The treaty with China took into account the temper of Californians and of Congress, but its aim was restriction not exclusion. Reformers were not entirely happy and spoilsmen were angered by Hayes's civil service policy, but he left the party machinery sufficiently intact to win in 1880. In addition, the experiment with the New York customhouse proved the feasibility of reform and made possible the passage of the 1883 Pendleton Civil Service Reform Act.

Hayes is also significant for the strikingly modern actions he took to enhance the power of the presidency. He defeated Republican senators over the so-called "courtesy of the Senate" convention and did not let them dictate appointments in the field service. He also defeated the Democratic congressional majority's stance toward the President's legislative role by not letting it destroy his veto power. In defeating the Democrats in the "Battle of the Riders," he relied on the power of public opinion, which he aroused in his stirring veto messages. Hayes traveled more widely than any previous President and, although he did not electioneer, he used every opportunity to speak on issues close to his heart. In this manner, he bypassed Congress to appeal directly to the people.

A Successful Politician

Historians have tended to echo the views of Republican Party leaders in the House and Senate that Hayes was an ineffective politician. Anything but an inept politician, Hayes shrewdly played presidential politics. He exploited issues and appealed to public opinion (which he viewed as the real government) by traveling widely and speaking often and briefly. Hayes knew that newspapers would pick up these talks and publicize his views. He also wrote his vetoes more for the public than for Congress, and by doing so vanquished the Democrats in the Battle of the Riders. Hayes was far more clever than the Conklings and Blaines, who turned on him when he refused to appoint their lieutenants to his cabinet and would not let them dominate his administration. They, especially Conkling, believed that organization based on patronage was the key to political success, while Hayes relied on what Theodore Roosevelt later called the "bully pulpit." Hayes was reform minded, but was aware of what was possible and avoided the impossible. His middle-of-the-road positions on issues like civil service reform and temperance kept the Republican Party together and strong enough to win in 1880, although reformers grumbled that he did not do enough, and spoilsmen howled that he was destroying their organizations. In fact, he introduced about all the reform that could be administered successfully without destroying Republican Party organizations.

Hayes's attitude toward temperance is a good example of the shrewdness of his middle path. Both Hayes and Lucy believed that, rather than coerce society not to drink, the public should be persuaded that drinking to excess is disreputable, if not dangerous. But he (not Lucy) banned liquor from the White House as much to gain political advantage as to set a good example and curb boorish behavior. He realized that temperance advocates in the Republican party would applaud his move and not flock to the Prohibitionists—a third party he disliked—and he knew that the wets would stay in the party since his symbolic act did little to hamper them. Hayes proved to be most perceptive on this point. His successors, James A. Garfield and Chester A. Arthur, brought wine back to the White House, the temperance people deserted the Republicans for the Prohibitionists and, because of their defection the Republicans, lost New York and the election to the Democrats in 1884.

Hayes did make a serious mistake, however, in refusing to run for reelection. With the economy rebounding and the Republicans united by the Battle of the Riders, he probably would have won. Presidents who serve only one term are usually written off as mediocrities, while those acclaimed as great have been reelected to a second term; a second term enables Presidents to implement more fully their policy initiatives. Four more years would have allowed Hayes to widen the application of civil service reform principles beyond the important New York offices. With a Republican Congress, he might well have enforced the election laws and protected black voters in the South. He was the last President in the nineteenth century who was genuinely interested in preserving voting rights for blacks.

Hayes was a respectable, dignified, and decent egalitarian. He had a sensitive nature, a judicious temperament, and a pragmatic attitude. He was a patient reformer who attempted what was possible and was optimistic that education of the public would accomplish in the future the present day impossibility. Shortly before he died Hayes concluded "I am 'a radical in thought (and principle) and a conservative in method' (and conduct)."

Made in the USA
Las Vegas, NV
07 December 2020